PHYLLIS E. JOHNS[illegible]

CW01646537

Gluten-free SCANDINAVIAN TREATS

MCP BOOKS

MCP Books
555 Winderley Pl, Suite 225
Maitland, FL 32751
407.339.4217
www.millcitypress.net

© 2024 by Phyllis E. Johnson, PhD

All rights reserved solely by the author. The author guarantees all contents are original and do not infringe upon the legal rights of any other person or work. No part of this book may be reproduced in any form without the permission of the author.

Due to the changing nature of the Internet, if there are any web addresses, links, or URLs included in this manuscript, these may have been altered and may no longer be accessible. The views and opinions shared in this book belong solely to the author and do not necessarily reflect those of the publisher. The publisher therefore disclaims responsibility for the views or opinions expressed within the work.

Paperback ISBN-13: 978-1-66289-730-6
Ebook ISBN-13: 978-1-66289-731-3

In memory of
Lillie, Mary, and Evelyn,
who taught me to bake.

TABLE OF CONTENTS

OTHER DESSERTS

QUICK BREADS AND FLATBREADS

ACKNOWLEDGMENTS

I owe a lot to my mother Evelyn Lanes and both grandmothers, Lillie Svaren and Mary Lanes. They taught me how to bake, and from them, I learned the finer points of some Scandinavian specialties. Recipes that I adapted to be gluten-free came from many sources, but especially those women, plus my mother-in-law Nettie Johnson and my first husband's aunts, Joná and Áugusta Johnson. Other recipes came from friends Ella Belling and Kari Brekke. A variety of church cookbooks were also helpful.

My daughter Sara Kenney got me started on this project when she had a boyfriend whose family couldn't eat gluten, and I had to figure out how to make gluten-free lefse for Thanksgiving dinner. My goddaughter and niece Amy and my grandson Alaric can't eat gluten, and they inspired much of the work reflected here.

Much of this work was done during the pandemic, and my late husband Bill Higdon was my chief taster and an enthusiastic cheerleader. Friends, especially Julie Evans, were happy to take the excess from my obsessive baking.

Special thanks to my daughter-in-law Robyn Johnson. She is both an excellent writer and a great cook. She edited all these recipes and made sure that the directions made sense.

My friend Dr. Sally Pyle took all the photos, for which I am very grateful.

INTRODUCTION

Why did I create this cookbook?

This project began when my daughter invited her gluten-free boyfriend and his family to Thanksgiving dinner. She asked if I could figure out how to make gluten-free lefse. As a retired scientist who used to study food science and human nutrition for the United States Department of Agriculture, I immediately tackled her request like a chemistry problem. After multiple experiments, I came up with a recipe that worked.

When I found out that several of my nieces and grandchildren also couldn't eat gluten, I decided to work on more recipes. As I continued to work on recipe development, I learned that gluten intolerance and celiac disease are common among people of Scandinavian descent, so the audience for my recipes is bigger than my family.

So, I decided to create this cookbook and concentrate on recipes for the Scandinavian goodies that many of us grew up with–those we especially enjoy on holidays and special occasions. I've also included a few recipes I have never seen published in commercial cookbooks. I chose to focus on cakes, cookies, and desserts to the exclusion of yeast breads.

I am of Norwegian and Swedish descent, and my first husband was of Icelandic descent. The majority of my recipes have their origins in those countries. However, many of these foods are common to all five Nordic countries (Norway, Sweden, Denmark, Finland, and Iceland).

What did I learn before creating the recipes?

When I began to develop my gluten-free recipes, I used a flour mixture from America's Test Kitchen. I learned, however, that most people don't want to purchase all the ingredients required to make their own flour mix. They would prefer to use a commercially available gluten-free flour.

My next decision was to test recipes with several commercial gluten-free flours that can be directly substituted for wheat flour. I did the testing so you don't have to!

While a one-for-one substitution will often work, I found that when using gluten-free flour, many recipes need modification. I also learned that some of the one-for-one flours perform differently in certain recipes.

Part of the difference comes from whether or not the gluten-free flours contain xanthan gum or acacia gum. These two ingredients are added to provide elasticity. They make the flour behave more like wheat and other flours with gluten.

I learned that gluten-free flours that are labeled *all-purpose* don't contain gums. In some recipes, such as sponge cake, an all-purpose, gluten-free flour *without* xanthan gum is desirable (see *Bløtkake,* for example). All-purpose flours also work fine for non-baked recipes that need flour—like gravy or white sauce. However, for most baked goods, xanthan gum needs to be added. Commercial gluten-free flours that say they can be substituted one-for-one in place of wheat flour have small amounts of xanthan gum or acacia gum added.

To help you use the recipes in this cookbook, I will simply call flours with added xanthan or acacia gum "one-for-one" flours. If a particular brand of one-for-one flour works better than another, I will note that.

Another reason that direct substitution of a gluten-free flour for wheat flour doesn't work as well as you would like is that each brand of flour contains a different mix of ingredients. Some of them contain relatively large amounts of cornstarch, for example, and that affects texture. Other brands have ingredients that affect color or flavor in some recipes.

My goal for this cookbook was to create gluten-free recipes that produce Scandinavian baked goods and desserts as good as food from "regular" recipes. If people can't tell the difference, then I'll know I've met my goal.

How did I create the recipes in this cookbook?

To achieve my goal, I tested each recipe with at least three gluten-free flours. I first made what, as a scientist, I call a "control" batch. That is, I made the recipe with regular wheat flour so I could compare the products from gluten and gluten-free flours.

I found that sometimes a gluten-free recipe needs adjustments in the amount of flour or other ingredients. I also found that sometimes the batter or dough needs to rest for a while to let the gluten-free flour absorb moisture from the wet ingredients. And I found that sometimes baking times are a bit different. Occasionally, it's necessary to add additional xanthan gum beyond what's included in the commercial flour blend.

As I experimented, I learned that each commercial gluten-free flour is a mixture of starches and other ingredients in varying proportions. The amount and type of ingredients make those commercial gluten-free flours different in how they work in recipes.

How can you quickly understand the differences among flours?

It can be a bit confusing to understand differences in gluten-free flours. I discovered that in the US, most wheat flour is fortified with iron and B vitamins, but most gluten-free flours are not.

However, the King Arthur brand does fortify its flours, so that for every thirty grams, approximately three tablespoons, there is a nutritionally meaningful amount of iron, thiamine, riboflavin, and niacin. If you need more iron in your diet, you might want to consider one of the flours with significant iron content.

As I made sense of flours on the market, I began creating tables showing the differences. I added two tables to this cookbook to help you quickly understand the differences among flours.

Table 1 shows ingredients for most common brands. You can quickly see which brands will work for your needs. For example, if you need a flour that doesn't contain milk or cornstarch, you can choose a brand without those ingredients.

Table 2 shows nutrients for each of the flours. You can again quickly use the table like you would the nutrition label on the package of flour. The nutrition labels are based on serving size. However, I found the brands in the table don't all define serving size the same way For some, serving size is three tablespoons; for others, it's four.

To make it easier for you to compare the nutrients, I based all the values in Table 2 on a serving size of about three tablespoons or thirty grams. For that reason, the numbers may look slightly different than they do on your package of flour. Hopefully, you'll find it easier to make comparisons and decide which is best for you.

Are there other gluten-free baking hints?

Many recipes call for greasing and flouring the pan. For "regular" baking, commercial cooking sprays with flour are handy. A substitute is needed for gluten-free baking, and this is especially true if using a fluted or other specially-shaped pan. Gluten-free batters seem to stick worse than "regular" versions of the same recipe. It's easy to make your own substitute for baking spray. I included a recipe for that too–*Gluten-Free Baking Pan Rub*.

Many recipes, such as lefse and some cookies, require rolling out the dough with a rolling pin. I find that this works best if I use a cloth-covered pastry board (like the one sold for making lefse) along with a rolling pin that's covered with a "sock" (look for these where you buy lefse-making equipment, too.) Both the pastry cloth and the rolling pin still need to be well-floured so that the dough doesn't stick.

Cardamom is a spice that is used in a lot of Scandinavian baking. Some people who don't care for it substitute cinnamon. If you do, the result won't be quite the same. Cardamom is expensive. So, to be sure it stays fresh, I store my bottle of ground cardamom in a heavy plastic bag in the freezer.

Oh, I have one more point. Recipes can be affected by the size of eggs. I tested all recipes in this cookbook with *large* eggs.

I hope you find this cookbook helpful as you prepare Scandinavian cake, cookie, and dessert recipes for those who must avoid gluten.

Gluten-Free Baking Pan Rub

Ingredients:

- ½ cup vegetable shortening
- ½ cup rice flour
- ½ cup vegetable oil

Instructions:

1. Mix the shortening and rice flour together and then add the vegetable oil. Beat until smooth.

2. Store in a jar at room temperature for up to three months. Apply to baking pans with a pastry brush or a wadded-up paper towel.

3. To make a version that won't leave a white residue on a chocolate cake such as Kladdekaka, substitute ½ cup cocoa for the rice flour.

Notes:

If you prefer to make this in smaller amounts as you go, just use equal amounts of the three ingredients; for example, a tablespoon of each.

Always combine the shortening and rice flour before adding oil. This avoids having lumps in the final product.

Cookies

Krumkaker

Crispy Cone Cookies

"Krumkake" means crumb cake in Norwegian. ("Krumkaker" is the plural.) These crispy cookies will indeed make lots of crumbs as soon as you bite into one. You can't make them on a damp day, or they will be soggy and tough. For a really decadent treat, fill with whipped cream and eat immediately (spray cans of cream are handy for this). I saw a picture once of krumkaker standing on end in a large bowl of sugar, filled with whipped cream, and topped with a whole strawberry.

If you can't find a krumkake iron, you can use a pizzelle iron (made for Italian cookies that are similar). If you have an old-fashioned iron that goes over a stove burner, you will need to turn the iron over to cook on the second side. With an electric iron (a marvelous invention!), both sides cook at once. Even with a non-stick electric krumkake iron, I find it helpful to use a bit of cooking spray on the surfaces before starting. Spray lightly, and then wipe off any excess with a paper towel before heating the iron.

3-4 dozen, depending on size of your iron.

❍ 4 eggs
❍ 1 cup sugar
❍ ½ cup butter, melted and cooled slightly
❍ 5 Tbsp cream
❍ 1 tsp vanilla
❍ ¾ cup one-for-one flour
❍ 2 tsp cornstarch
❍ 2 tsp xanthan gum (SEE NOTE)

Melt butter and let it cool. Beat eggs and sugar together thoroughly, then add butter, cream, and vanilla. Blend flour, cornstarch, and xanthan gum and mix into the egg mixture. Beat until smooth. Heat krumkake iron until hot enough for a drop of water to "jump." Drop batter from the spoon onto the iron, close it, and bake until krumkake is a light, golden brown. This takes about one minute on my electric krumkake iron, which has no heat adjustment. Adjust timing as needed for your iron. Remove with a table knife and roll around a wooden krumkake cone while warm. Let cool and remove from form. Store in a dry place.

NOTE: Although one-for-one flours list acacia gum or xanthan gum as ingredients in their flour mix, it is not enough, and you still need to add the xanthan gum called for in this recipe. If you don't, the batter will be extremely runny, the krumkake will stick to the iron, and they will be unacceptably fragile. Cornstarch helps make the krumkaker crisp.

Spritz

Pressed Butter Cookies

In my family, spritz are absolutely necessary for celebrating Christmas. My dad was the spritz maker, although he left most other baking to my mom. This recipe is from his mother.

Spritz can be made any time of year, of course. Most cookie presses come with multiple dies that will produce all kinds of seasonal shapes. Sometimes people add food coloring to the dough or sprinkle them with colored sugar before baking.

About 5 dozen cookies
Oven: 400°F

- ❍ 1 cup butter, softened
- ❍ ½ cup sugar
- ❍ 1 egg
- ❍ ½ tsp salt
- ❍ 1 ½ tsp almond extract
- ❍ 2 ¼ cups one-for-one flour (SEE NOTE)

Preheat the oven to 400°F. Mix butter, sugar, egg, salt, and almond extract thoroughly. Add flour and mix very well. This works best in a stand mixer. Fill cookie press with dough and extrude cookies onto **ungreased** baking sheet. Bake for 8-9 minutes until just barely brown on the edges. Let cool for a minute or two on the baking sheet before transferring to a cooling rack.

Don't use parchment on your cookie sheet. The dough needs to adhere to the cookie sheet when it comes out of the cookie press. Use a bare, ungreased cookie sheet.

Don't chill the dough. If it isn't at room temperature, it will be impossible to extrude it through the cookie press.

NOTE: I do not recommend Cup4Cup or Bob's Red Mill 1:1 flour for this recipe. Spritz made with Cup4Cup browned more than spritz made with other flours, and they had a powdery texture that was unlike regular spritz, most likely because of the high cornstarch content of the flour. Bob's Red Mill flour produced spritz that weren't as white, and there was a slight flavor of garbanzo beans that came through despite the almond extract.

Sandbakkels

Sand Tarts

This is adapted from a recipe I've used for decades. It came from a 1950's era church cookbook that my Swedish grandmother's congregation published. The recipe, from a Mrs. Carl Nelson (women didn't use first names publicly then!), is old enough that the list of ingredients ends with "enough flour." They just assumed everyone knew how the dough should turn out. It didn't specify a baking temperature or time either because the recipe came from the days when many people still cooked on woodstoves. I always think of my grandma when I make these.

Sandbakkel tins are tiny, fluted tart pans that come in various shapes–round, diamond, shell. Most people serve these cookies upside down to show off the fluting better. You can also use them as tart shells, with a few berries and a spoonful of whipped cream inside. This is another recipe kids like to help with.

About 2 ½ dozen
Oven: 350°F

- ❍ 1 cup butter, softened
- ❍ ½ cup sugar
- ❍ 2 eggs
- ❍ 1 tsp almond extract
- ❍ ½ tsp salt
- ❍ 2 ½ cups one-for-one flour (SEE NOTE)

Cream butter and sugar, then beat in eggs, almond extract, and salt. Add flour and mix well. Press dough evenly into ungreased sandbakkel tins. Make sure that the dough doesn't lap over the top of the tins, or it will be impossible to get the cookies out when they are baked. Place tins on a cookie sheet and bake for 12-14 minutes until just lightly brown. Slide the tins onto a cooling rack after removing from the oven and let them cool about

5 minutes, then turn them over and remove the cookies by tapping lightly on the cooling rack. Makes about 2 ½ dozen.

NOTE: If using Bob's Red Mill 1:1 flour, add 2 Tbsp cornstarch. Potato starch will produce an acceptable cookie but not quite as crisp as those made with cornstarch. If you use Good and Gather, add 2 Tbsp more flour. I do not recommend using Domata or Good & Gather for this recipe. Domata flour, which has cornstarch as its second most abundant ingredient, did not make satisfactory cookies; they were almost chewy. With Good and Gather flour, the millet flavor seemed to overwhelm the almond flavor.

Fattigman

Poor Man's Cookie

My Aunt Gene was the fattigman maker in our extended family, and I remember eating wonderful fattigman at her house. Fattigman are light and crisp, in contrast to the heavier, chewier Icelandic Kleinur, which are the same shape and also deep-fried. Fattigman means "poor man" in Norwegian. This is a traditional Christmas cookie in Norway. Many Scandinavian shops sell fattigman cutters that will automatically cut the dough the correct shape.

About 3 dozen cookies

- ❍ 3 egg yolks
- ❍ 1 whole egg
- ❍ ½ tsp salt
- ❍ ¼ c powdered sugar
- ❍ 1 tsp vanilla
- ❍ 1 ½ tsp xanthan gum (SEE NOTE)
- ❍ 1 ¼ cup one-for-one flour
- ❍ Oil for frying

Heat oil to 375°F. Mix flour and xanthan gum together. In another bowl, mix egg yolks, egg, and salt and beat until very stiff. With a stand mixer, this takes about 10 minutes. Add sugar and vanilla and mix well. Chill for 30 minutes. Take half the dough, place it on a floured surface, and pat it into a disk. Then roll into a 12–14" circle. Cut into diamond shapes about 2" on a side and make a slit in the middle. If you have a fattigman cutter, simply use that. Form into knots by putting the tail of the diamond through the center slit. Fry in several inches of oil at 375°F for about a minute until golden brown. Drain on paper towels. Sprinkle with sugar or powdered sugar to serve.

NOTE: This is a recipe that requires extra xanthan gum in addition to what's in the one-for-one flour. Without it, it's impossible to roll out the dough.

Rosetter

Rosettes

Rosettes are a deep-fried treat that I associate with Christmas, although they are good any time. They are thin and crisp. Don't make these very far ahead of serving. They will get soggy quickly if there is any humidity in the air. Most rosette irons will make two cookies at a time.

Be sure to use oil that hasn't been used for frying other kinds of food so that the rosettes don't pick up unwanted flavors. On a trip to Yugoslavia once, I bought rosettes from a vendor on the street. They were rather spicy because the Pakistani woman who sold them had evidently cooked something else in the oil before she made the rosettes.

Makes about 18

- ½ cup one-for-one flour
- 1 Tbsp sugar
- ½ tsp salt
- ½ cup milk
- 1 egg, slightly beaten
- 1 Tbsp vegetable oil
- Cooking oil for frying
- Powdered sugar

Heat oil to 375°F. Mix the dry ingredients together. Mix the egg, milk, and oil, and then stir in the dry ingredients. Put the batter through a wire-mesh strainer to remove any lumps. Pour it into a container just large enough to hold the rosette iron when it's dipped in. A small loaf pan works well for this. Heat the rosette iron in the oil, dip into the batter just far enough so batter comes about ¾ of the way up the side of the iron, and then fry until brown. This will take only about 30 seconds. Gently tap the cooked rosette with a knife to dislodge it; drain on paper towels. Heat the iron again before making the next one, and drain briefly on a paper towel. If the iron is too cold, the batter will slip off into the oil; if it's too hot, the batter will stick to the iron. The reason to use a container just big enough for the iron to fit into is so that the batter will be as deep as possible; that way, you can dip into it to make the maximum number of rosettes. Sprinkle the rosettes with powdered sugar just before serving.

Hvite Nøtter

White Nuts Tea Cakes

This cookie is very similar to what many know as Russian Teacakes or Mexican Wedding Cakes but shaped into cylinders instead of balls. The recipe came from a family friend whose dad emigrated from Norway in the 1960s.

Makes about 4 dozen
Oven: 375°F

- ❍ 1 cup butter, at room temperature (SEE NOTE)
- ❍ ¼ cup powdered sugar
- ❍ 1 tsp water
- ❍ 1 tsp vanilla
- ❍ 2 cups one-for-one flour
- ❍ 1 tsp xanthan gum (SEE NOTE)
- ❍ 1 cup chopped nuts (pecans or walnuts)
- ❍ Powdered sugar for rolling

Cream butter and sugar thoroughly. Add water and vanilla and mix in until combined. Beat in flour and xanthan gum until the dough starts to form itself into a ball. Stir in nuts.

Shape into cylinders the size of a date (about two teaspoons of dough). Bake on parchment-covered cookie sheet for 15 minutes. Cookies will be just barely starting to brown. Slip the parchment onto a cooling rack and let sit for five minutes until they are cool enough to handle. Roll in powdered sugar while still warm.

NOTE: Make sure the butter is soft; otherwise, the dough may be dry and crumbly after the flour is mixed in. Adding extra liquid at that point will only make the cookies crumbly after baking. This recipe requires xanthan gum in addition to what's in the flour. Without any egg to bind the flour and butter together, the extra xanthan gum is essential to keep these cookies from falling apart before they are even rolled in the powdered sugar. Sliding the parchment onto the cooling rack results in less jostling to the cookies that are fragile while warm.

Kleinur

Icelandic Donuts

This recipe is from my husband's Aunt Jóna. It's an old Icelandic snack that Bob called "Icelandic donuts," but kleinur are chewier than American cake donuts. They are the same shape as Norwegian fattigman, but fattigman are thin and crisp, while kleinur are thicker and a bit chewy. This is half of Jóna's original recipe, which made twelve or thirteen dozen Kleinur (the word means "little one"). The recipe dates back to the time when farming was done with horses and involved heavy manual labor, so a farm crew needed lots to eat. Jóna used lard to fry these, but vegetable oil is a healthier option. Every single kleinur will come out a slightly different shape after hitting the hot fat.

About 6 dozen

- ❍ 3 eggs
- ❍ 1 cup sugar
- ❍ 1 cup milk
- ❍ ½ cup cream
- ❍ ¾ tsp baking powder
- ❍ ⅔ tsp ground cardamom
- ❍ 4 ½ cup one-for-one flour
- ❍ 1 ½ tsp xanthan gum
- ❍ 2 ½ tsp salt
- ❍ Oil for deep frying
- ❍ Granulated sugar

Mix the eggs and sugar, and then mix in the milk and cream. Add the baking powder, cardamom, xanthan gum, and salt to the first cup of flour so it gets mixed in well. Stir in flour a cup at a time to make a stiff dough. Chill the dough for at least 30 minutes. Heat the oil to 375°F. Roll and cut with a fattigman cutter or a knife into diamond shapes about 2" on a side and make a slit in the middle. Push the tail of each diamond through the slit in the middle before dropping into the hot oil. If they tend to break when you put the end through the slit, try re-rolling the dough with just a tad more flour. Fry until golden. Cool and dredge in granulated sugar if desired.

Berliner Kranser

Berlin Wreaths

Despite the name, this is a very Norwegian cookie, traditionally one of the seven kinds of cookies that a proper Norwegian Christmas cookie plate should have. My mother-in-law used to make these every December. The recipe is unusual because it contains hard-boiled egg yolks, which contribute to the cookie's light texture. The other unusual thing is the order that the ingredients are mixed. Instead of creaming the butter and sugar together first, then adding eggs, and then flour, the butter and flour are added alternately at the end. This ensures that every last bit of flour gets coated by the butter, helping give these cookies their light, melt-in-your-mouth texture.

Makes 4 dozen
Oven: 350°F

- ❍ 2 hard-boiled egg yolks
- ❍ 2 eggs, separated
- ❍ ⅔ cup sugar
- ❍ 1 tsp ground cardamom *or* the grated zest of one orange
- ❍ 1 cup butter (2 sticks) at room temperature
- ❍ 2 ¼ cups one-for-one flour
- ❍ Pearl sugar for sprinkling
- ❍ Optional: bits of red or green candied fruit for decorating the wreaths

Mix the cardamom or zest with the flour and set aside. Mash the hard-boiled egg yolks with a fork. Add the raw egg yolks and mix until they are thoroughly combined. Add the sugar and beat until the mixture is light and fluffy. Cut the butter into 8 chunks. Add the butter and about ¼ cup flour alternately, mixing well after each addition until a smooth dough comes together. Cover and chill for half an hour. If you chill it much longer, let the dough warm up for half an hour or more before you try to work it.

Take a portion of the dough and roll it with your hands into a rope no bigger around than a pencil. Cut a length of 5-6″ and shape into a circle or a **Q** shape on a parchment-lined cookie pan. Chill the pan of cookies for 10-15 minutes before baking. Meanwhile, beat the egg whites lightly. Brush the chilled cookies with the egg white and sprinkle with the pearl sugar. Bake for about 10 minutes until just barely turning brown. Leave the cookies on the parchment and set on a rack to cool. They are extremely fragile while warm and will crisp up as they cool. These keep for several days, and they can also be frozen.

Hestesko

Norwegian Horseshoe Cookies

This is a recipe I got from my friend Ella when our kids were in a Norwegian folk dance group together, and she made these cookies for them. It's a recipe she brought with her when she emigrated from Norway to the US. I've never seen this in any cookbook. It's a recipe that kids enjoy helping with as they shape the dough into horseshoes.

About 5 dozen
Oven: 350°F

- ❍ ¾ cup butter, softened
- ❍ ¾ cup sugar
- ❍ 1 egg
- ❍ 1 ¾ cups one-for-one flour
- ❍ 1 ½ Tbsp dark corn syrup
- ❍ 1 tsp cardamom
- ❍ 2 tsp cinnamon
- ❍ 2 tsp baking soda
- ❍ Dash of pepper

Mix flour, soda, and spices. In a separate bowl, cream the butter and sugar, and then beat in the egg and corn syrup. Add the flour mixture and mix until well combined.

On a lightly floured surface, roll out portions of dough into ropes about the diameter of a pencil or less. Cut into pieces about 4" long. Place each piece on a parchment-lined cookie sheet and shape into a wide U or horseshoe shape. Press with a lightly floured fork. Bake for 8–10 minutes until barely browned. Slide the parchment onto a cooling rack and let the cookies cool before you remove them from the parchment. They will be crisp when cool but are tender when warm, which makes it easier to move the entire parchment than individual cookies.

Pepperkaker

Norwegian spice cookies

This recipe is adapted from one published by the Royal Norwegian Embassy many years ago. "Pepperkaker" literally means "pepper cookies." Some recipes for these cookies actually contain a bit of black pepper, but I prefer this mixture of spices. There is a lot of ginger in this recipe, which would taste hotter if not mellowed by the other warm spices.

When I was growing up, every church cookbook had a section for Refrigerator Cookies, Icebox Cookies, or Overnight Cookies. Slicing chilled rolls of dough is a quick and easy way to make cookies, and it's an option with this dough. However, this dough is traditionally rolled out thin and cut with cookie cutters. The thin, crisp rolled cookies are among those often made at Christmas time throughout Scandinavia.

Makes about 6 dozen cookies when rolled, fewer if dough is sliced.
Oven: 350°F

- ❍ 1 cup butter
- ❍ ¾ cup sugar
- ❍ ⅔ cup dark corn syrup
- ❍ 1 tsp ground cardamom
- ❍ 1 Tbsp ground ginger
- ❍ 1 tsp ground cloves
- ❍ 3 Tbsp cinnamon
- ❍ 1 tsp baking soda
- ❍ 2 eggs
- ❍ 1 cup chopped almonds (optional)
- ❍ 4 cups one-for-one flour (SEE NOTE)

Melt butter over low heat, and add corn syrup, sugar, spices, soda, and almonds. Remove from heat and pour into the bowl of a stand mixer. Let cool to lukewarm and mix in eggs. Mix in flour. Put half the dough onto a sheet of plastic wrap and form into a cylinder about two inches in diameter. Repeat with other half of dough. Chill overnight unless you are using Namaste flour. (See note.)

For traditional Christmas cookies, roll the dough very thin and cut with cookie cutters. Bake on greased or parchment-lined cookie sheets for 6–8 minutes. Alternatively, the rolls of dough can be sliced and baked for about 10–12 minutes.

NOTE: Namaste flour contains arrowroot flour, which has double the thickening power of most other starches used in gluten-free flours, so it makes a rather stiff dough. If you use Namaste, chill only for an hour or two before making rolled cookies.

Hallongrotter

Hazelnut Raspberry Thumbprint Cookies

The "hallon" in the Swedish name for these cookies refers to raspberries, and "grott" to caves or grottos. So, you could also call these Raspberry Caves. The paper cups sold for making bite-size muffins work perfectly to help these tender cookies keep their shape during baking.

Makes about 2 ½ dozen
Oven: 350°F

- ❍ ¾ cup roasted hazelnuts
- ❍ 1 cup one-for-one flour
- ❍ ⅛ tsp salt
- ❍ ½ cup butter, at room temperature
- ❍ ⅓ cup sugar
- ❍ 1 egg yolk
- ❍ ½ tsp vanilla
- ❍ ¼ tsp almond extract
- ❍ ½ cup seedless raspberry jam or preserves
- ❍ Mini paper baking cups

Process hazelnuts with flour and salt in a food processor until finely ground. Cream butter and sugar until light and fluffy, around 3 minutes. Add egg yolk, vanilla, and almond extract; mix until well combined. Add flour-nut mixture and mix on low until just combined.

Roll dough into tablespoon-sized balls and place into paper baking cups set on a cookie sheet. A one-tablespoon cookie scoop is perfect for this. Using a slightly floured finger or the back of a rounded half-teaspoon measuring spoon, press the center of each dough ball to make a well.

Bake for about 15 minutes or until just brown on the edges. Right after you take the cookies out of the oven, reinforce the well by pressing again because the dough will have puffed up a little. Cool on the baking sheet for 5 minutes and then transfer to a cooling rack.

If you don't have seedless jam, press it through a sieve to remove the seeds. Stir to an even consistency, heating for a few seconds in the microwave if necessary. Spoon jam into the center of the cooled cookies. Allow to cool completely before serving. Sprinkle with powdered sugar if desired.

<u>Variation:</u> Fill with Nutella instead of jam.

Norsk Mandelkake

Norwegian Almond Bars

This is an old recipe I found among my mother's things and one I have never seen in a cookbook. If you need to bring a pan of bars somewhere, you can't go wrong with these.

About 24 servings
Oven: 325°F

- ❍ 1 cup butter, softened
- ❍ 1 ½ cups sugar
- ❍ 1 egg plus one egg yolk
- ❍ 1 tsp almond extract
- ❍ 2 ½ cups one-for-one flour
- ❍ 1 egg white, slightly beaten
- ❍ ¾ to 1 cup sliced almonds
- ❍ Pearl sugar to sprinkle on top

Cream butter and sugar together, then beat in egg, egg yolk, and almond extract. Add flour and beat well until dough forms into a ball. Press the dough into a 9″ x 13″ rectangular pan or two 9″ cake pans. Brush with beaten egg white. Sprinkle sliced almonds on top and then sprinkle with pearl sugar. Bake for 30 minutes. When cool, slice into bars and serve. Cover tightly to store.

Bestemors Sukkerkjeks

Grandma's Sugar Cookies

This recipe came from my Grandma Lanes. It makes the most delicate sugar cookies I've ever eaten. The combination of almond and nutmeg is unusual and very tasty. You can re-roll the scraps more than a couple of times, but they will have so much flour in them that they will taste like store cookies. I prefer to roll out the dough on a floured pastry cloth rather than just a floured counter. The dough is less likely to stick, and it can be rolled really thin.

6-8 dozen cookies, depending on size of cookie cutters
Oven: 375°F

❍ 1 cup butter (2 sticks), softened
❍ 1 cup sugar
❍ 2 eggs
❍ 1 tsp almond extract
❍ ¼ cup milk
❍ ½ tsp salt
❍ 1 tsp baking soda
❍ ½ tsp nutmeg
❍ 2 tsp baking powder
❍ 3 cups one-for-one flour (SEE NOTE)

Stir together the flour, salt, soda, baking powder, and nutmeg in a bowl and set aside. In another bowl, cream the butter and sugar well, and then add the eggs and almond extract. Add half the flour mixture and blend well. Mix in the milk and then the remaining flour mixture. Dough will be stiff. Chill for at least half an hour.

Roll a portion of the dough on a floured surface, using a rolling pin with a well-floured "sock" on it. Keep the rest of the dough in the fridge until you need it. Cut out cookies and transfer to greased cookie sheets. Sprinkle with sugar, if desired, or leave plain if you want to frost them. Bake for 5-8 minutes until just slightly golden. Remove from pan and cool on wire rack. Frost if desired. You can re-roll the scraps a couple of times before they get too tough to make nice cookies.

NOTE: I do not recommend using Bob's Red Mill 1:1 flour for this recipe. The garbanzo bean flavor covers up the delicate flavor of these cookies.

Chokladsnittar

Swedish Chocolate Slices

These cookies taste a lot like American brownies, but they are drier and crisper. The texture is similar to Italian biscotti, but biscotti are baked twice. These are perfect for dunking in your coffee.

Makes 3-4 dozen
Oven: 400°F

- ❍ ¾ cup butter, softened
- ❍ 1 cup sugar
- ❍ 1 egg
- ❍ 2 cups one-for-one flour
- ❍ ¼ cup cocoa
- ❍ 1 tsp baking powder
- ❍ 1 ½ tsp vanilla

<u>Topping</u>

- ❍ 1 egg, whisked with 1 Tbsp water
- ❍ Pearl sugar

Cream the butter and sugar together until fluffy, and then mix in the egg and vanilla. Mix the other dry ingredients together in a separate bowl and then add them to the butter and eggs mixture. The dough will be rather stiff. Divide the dough into six portions, and shape each into a log about 8-9" long. Place on two greased or parchment-covered baking sheets and flatten them slightly with your hands or a small rolling pin. Brush lightly with the beaten egg and sprinkle with pearl sugar. Bake for 15 minutes. When you remove the pan from the oven, slice the logs on the diagonal into pieces about ¾" wide. Then let the cookies cool on the pan.

Smörkammar

Butter Combs

I found this recipe on a forgotten box of pearl sugar in the back of my cupboard. The box had a picture of these cookies along with the recipe–but the recipe was in Swedish! I haven't studied Swedish, but I know Norwegian, and I have a good dictionary, so I managed to translate the recipe. Being a baker helped too, because foreign language dictionaries often don't include cooking and baking terms. Apparently, I made the right guesses because the cookies turned out well after I converted metric measurements to English ones and Celsius to Fahrenheit.

The ratio of butter to all other ingredients in these delicate cookies is higher than in any other recipe I've ever seen. They are basically a delicious delivery system for butter.

Makes about 1 ½ dozen cookies
Oven: 425°F

- ❍ ⅔ cup butter (11 Tbsp)
- ❍ 1 cup + 1 Tbsp one-for-one flour
- ❍ 2 Tbsp powdered sugar
- ❍ 3-4 Tbsp cream
- ❍ 1 egg, beaten
- ❍ Pearl sugar for sprinkling

Put the flour, powdered sugar, and butter in the bowl of a food processor. Pulse until the mixture resembles small crumbs. Add the cream and pulse until a ball of dough forms. Chill for at least one hour. Roll out about ¼" thick. Cut into pieces about 1" x 2". Slide a knife under each cookie and transfer it to a sheet of parchment on a baking sheet. Create the teeth of the comb by making three cuts about ¾ of the way through on the long side of each cookie. Brush with beaten egg and sprinkle with pearl sugar. Chill the cookies for 10–15 minutes before baking. This will keep the butter in the cookies from melting and running out when they are baked.

Bake for about 9 minutes or until nicely browned. Any scraps of dough need to be chilled before re-rolling. Transfer the baked cookies, still on parchment, to a cooling rack and cool completely. The cookies are extremely fragile while warm but will crisp up as they cool.

Havreflarn
Oat Crisps

This is a quick and easy cookie that requires no more than a spoon to mix it up. From start to finish takes less than forty-five minutes. These popular cookies are sold at IKEA, the well-known Swedish store. The cookies IKEA sells have been dipped in chocolate, and chocolate-dipped cookies are definitely yummy, but I prefer them without chocolate. If you do decide to dip them, dark chocolate is a better contrast with these sweet cookies than milk chocolate.

Makes 18–22 cookies
Oven: 425°F

- ⅓ cup butter, melted
- 1 ⅛ cups quick-cooking oatmeal (SEE NOTE)
- ⅔ cup sugar
- 1 egg, lightly beaten
- 1 Tbsp gluten-free flour, with or without xanthan gum
- 1 tsp baking powder
- 3–4 oz melted chocolate for dipping (optional)

Pour the melted butter over the oatmeal and stir until mixed. Let it cool. Stir in sugar and egg. Add flour and baking powder and stir thoroughly. Using a #60 cookie scoop (1 Tbsp), put six dollops on each parchment-lined cookie pan. Make sure they are well-spaced because cookies will spread. Bake for 6 minutes until edges of cookies are brown and there is minimal bubbling in the middle. Slide parchment to a cooling rack. If desired, dip cooled cookies halfway into melted chocolate, place on wax paper, and chill in the refrigerator until chocolate is set.

NOTE: Don't use old-fashioned oatmeal or steel-cut oats for this recipe. The oats don't soften enough in the melted butter, and the cookies turn out excessively chewy because the oats aren't completely cooked through.

Cakes

Vínarterta/Vienetarta

Icelandic Prune Torte

Vínarterta is a cake made of cookie-like layers with a cardamom-spiced prune filling in between. It was at the height of its popularity in Iceland 120 years ago when many Icelanders immigrated to North America; it's less common in Iceland today. The name literally means "Vienna Cake." Prunes were the filling preferred by our immigrant ancestors because dried fruit was available in the winter. Layers are very thin because baking with a woodstove meant it was easier to get consistent results with thin layers rather than thicker ones. Modern Icelanders also use rhubarb or apricot jam as fillings.

In North America, Vínarterta is one of those things that shows up at weddings, funeral lunches, and Thanksgiving and Christmas. It's great for a coffee break on an ordinary day, too.

This recipe is based on one that I got from my husband's aunt Jóna. Her recipe did not contain cardamom in the cookie layers, but many recipes do. I've added some cardamom for a bit more flavor.

Serves 20
Oven: 400°F

Cookie Layers

- ❍ 1 cup sugar
- ❍ ½ cup butter, softened
- ❍ 2 eggs
- ❍ ½ cup milk
- ❍ 2 tsp baking powder
- ❍ 1 tsp salt
- ❍ 1 tsp ground cardamom
- ❍ 3 ½ to 4 cups one-for-one flour

Prune Filling

- 2 lb pitted prunes
- ½ cup sugar
- ½ tsp ground cardamom

Mix dry ingredients in a separate bowl and set aside. Cream the butter and sugar. Add eggs and beat well. Add half the dry ingredients, mix, then add the milk. Mix well and add the remaining dry ingredients. Mix to make a soft dough. Chill for 30-60 minutes.

Tape a piece of parchment paper to your counter. Take about ⅛ of the dough and pat it into a flat, round shape. Put a bit of flour on the outside of the dough patty. Roll out until large enough to cut a 7" circle, using a small plate as a template. Cut away excess dough and brush any loose flour away. Un-tape the parchment and slide it onto a baking sheet. Bake for about 6 minutes until just barely getting brown. Repeat until the dough is used up. Slide the parchment onto a rack to cool. Some people prefer to make square cakes, about 8" x 8".

To prepare the filling, cover the prunes with water and cook until soft. Process in a food processor to make a paste. Return the prunes to the saucepan, add sugar and cardamom, and heat until the sugar dissolves. Stir while heating to prevent burning. Cool to room temperature. This makes about 4 cups of filling.

To assemble the cake, first pick out the nicest cookie layer to save for the top. Place a cookie layer on a plate, spread thickly with about ⅓ cup of the prune jam, add another layer, and continue until the cake is as tall as you want it or all the cookie layers are used up. I find that with more than five or six cookie layers, it's so tall that the slices fall apart when it's cut, but I know people who think seven or eight layers are the way to do it. Wrap the cake tightly in plastic wrap or foil and let sit at room temperature for a couple of days so that moisture from the filling penetrates the cookie layers. This freezes well.

To serve, cut into strips about half an inch wide. Then cut the strips into pieces 1-2 inches long. Lay on a plate so that the stripes show.

Bløtkake

Norwegian Strawberries and Cream Cake

Bløtkake (which literally means "wet cake") is a cake for celebrations. It's a cake for the 17th of May (Norway's Constitution Day), for birthdays, special family reunions, and the like. Cookbooks written in English usually name it "Strawberries and Cream Cake," but it's more elaborate than our American strawberry shortcake. It can be made with other fruits, too, especially if strawberries are out of season. I had a Norwegian friend who put drained, canned peach slices and other fruit on top and used apricot jam in the filling. On the 17th of May, the decorative fruit on top might be both strawberries and blueberries, arranged in the shape of the cross on the Norwegian flag.

When I visited my father's cousins in Haugesund, they served Bløtkake. To serve, they cut a round section in the middle, and then cut slices from the outside. The rationale was that if you didn't eat up all the cake, you would still have a nice round section from the middle.

Serves 12-16
Oven: 350°F

Cake

- ❍ 1 ¼ cups gluten-free flour without xanthan gum
- ❍ 2 tsp baking powder
- ❍ ⅜ tsp salt
- ❍ ⅓ cup milk
- ❍ 3 ½ Tbsp butter
- ❍ ¾ tsp vanilla
- ❍ 8 eggs (4 separated, 4 whole)
- ❍ 1 ¼ cups sugar, divided into two portions of ⅝ cup each (½ cup + 2 Tbsp).

Custard Filling

- ❍ 3 egg yolks
- ❍ 2 Tbsp butter
- ❍ 2 Tbsp cornstarch, sifted to remove any lumps
- ❍ ¼ cup sugar
- ❍ ¾ cup milk
- ❍ ¾ cup whipping cream (or use 1 ½ cups half and half instead of milk + cream)
- ❍ 2 tsp vanilla

Other

- ❍ ⅓ cup strawberry jam
- ❍ 1 pint strawberries
- ❍ ¾ cup whipping cream, whipped with 1 Tbsp sugar until it makes peaks

Butter three 9″ cake pans or grease with Gluten-Free Pan Rub and also line them with parchment. Place the oven rack just below the middle of the oven. Heat milk and butter together, add vanilla, and cover to keep warm. Mix the flour, baking powder, and salt together in a small bowl and set aside.

Separate 4 of the eggs and put the whites in one large mixer bowl and the yolks in another. Add the 4 remaining whole eggs to the bowl with the yolk and set aside. Beat the whites until they form soft, glossy peaks, adding half of the sugar as you beat them. Set aside. Beat the whole eggs and yolks with the other half of the sugar until they become thick and very pale yellow; they will double in volume. Add the yolk mixture to the whites and fold together gently. Sprinkle the flour mixture onto the eggs and fold in with about a dozen strokes. Make a little well on one side of the batter and pour the milk/butter mixture into it. Fold until all is combined, but do not overmix. Divide the batter into the three prepared pans. Bake for about 16 minutes until light brown and the cake springs back when touched. Cool on a rack for 5 minutes and then remove the layers from the pans and let cool completely.

For the custard filling, mix all ingredients except vanilla in a small saucepan. Sift the cornstarch into the mixture to ensure there won't be any lumps. Cook over medium heat, constantly whisking until the mixture is thick and smooth.

Remove from heat and cool slightly. Stir in vanilla, cover with plastic, and chill in the refrigerator before assembling the cake.

To assemble

Place one layer on the cake plate. Warm the strawberry jam in the microwave for about 30 seconds, mash any large pieces of strawberry, and spread onto the first layer. Top with thinly sliced strawberries. Put the next layer on top and cover it with the chilled custard. Top with the last layer. Cover the top of the cake with whipped cream and top with halved strawberries for decoration. Chill for about an hour before cutting.

Mandelkaka

Swedish Almond Cake

Most Scandinavian specialty stores sell special pans for this cake. They are about 4 1/2″ x 12″ with a round, fluted bottom. Once you turn the cake out of the pan, you have a pretty, fluted cake, and you can slice it on the indentations. The same stores usually also have rectangular trays just the right size for this cake. This is very much like a pound cake. It freezes well. If you want to make this cake but don't have the special pan, you will need a fairly small loaf pan. The specialty pan only holds about three cups of batter, which is what this recipe makes.

Serves about 18
Oven: 350°F

- ❍ 1 ¼ cup sugar
- ❍ 1 egg
- ❍ 1 ½ tsp almond extract
- ❍ ⅔ cup milk
- ❍ 1 ¼ cup one-for-one flour
- ❍ ½ tsp baking powder
- ❍ ½ cup butter, melted and cooled
- ❍ 2 Tbsp sliced almonds for topping (optional)

Grease and flour the pan. If desired, sprinkle the bottom of the pan with the sliced almonds.

Beat the sugar, egg, almond extract, and milk together. Add the flour and baking powder; mix well. Add melted butter and mix well. Bake at 350°F for about 40 minutes. The top of the cake should be golden brown, and a toothpick inserted in the middle should come out clean. Cool in the pan on a rack until completely cool. The cake will stick or break if removed too soon. When cool, turn the cake out onto a plate. This looks nice with a little powdered sugar dusted on top.

Kladdekaka

Sticky Cake

I had never heard of Kladdekaka until I saw a pan with a recipe at my local Scandinavian shop. Since I'm a sucker for both new recipes and new gadgets, I had to get it. A Kladdekaka pan is a round eight-inch pan with a fluted edge, and it's raised in the middle. When the cake is turned out on a plate, there is a ridge around the outside edge. The cake is similar to a brownie, but interestingly, it contains no baking powder or other leavening except the air incorporated during mixing. It looks pretty made in the fancy pan. This can also be baked in an eight-inch round cake pan.

Serves 8
Oven: 350°F

- ½ cup butter, softened
- 1 ⅓ cups sugar
- 1 tsp vanilla
- ⅛ tsp salt
- ¼ cup unsweetened cocoa powder
- 2 eggs
- ½ cup one-for-one flour

Coat pan with Gluten-Free Pan Rub with Cocoa. Cream sugar, vanilla, salt, and cocoa with the butter. Add eggs and stir until smooth. Stir in flour until combined.

Bake on the lower rack of the oven for 25–30 minutes. Allow cake to cool in pan 15–20 minutes. Invert onto a plate. Dust with powdered sugar. Serve with whipped cream or ice cream. This is nice with fresh raspberries too.

The cake will firm up around the edges but still be very soft in the center when done. The center will puff up and look crackly. It won't spring back in the center when touched like a regular cake, but a toothpick inserted in the middle will come out clean. If you overbake it, the edges will get kind of hard. The cake typically falls in the middle when it cools.

Verdens Beste Kake

World's Best Cake

This cake is also called Kvæfjord cake. Kvæfjord is in the north of Norway in the district of Troms og Finnmark. In 2002, this cake was named Norway's national cake by a Norwegian TV entertainment show. It even has its own Wikipedia entry!

What to do with the other half of the pastry cream, you ask? One option is to make two cakes! Given the odd number of eggs in the pastry cream recipe, it's impossible to cut the recipe in half. The pastry cream is good on fresh berries as well as a filling for any other kind of cake. You can also freeze the other half of the pastry cream and eat it like ice cream.

Serves 8
Oven: 325°F

<u>Cake</u>

- ❍ 1 cup butter, softened
- ❍ ¼ cup + 1 ½ tsp sugar
- ❍ 5 egg yolks
- ❍ 1 tsp vanilla
- ❍ 1 cup one-for-one flour
- ❍ 1 tsp baking powder
- ❍ 3 ½ Tbsp milk

<u>Meringue</u>

- ❍ 5 egg whites
- ❍ Pinch of cream of tartar
- ❍ 1 cup sugar
- ❍ 1 cup sliced almonds

Filling
- ❍ ½ recipe pastry cream (see below)
- ❍ ⅓ cup cream

Pastry Cream
- ❍ 1 egg yolk
- ❍ 1 whole egg
- ❍ ¼ cup cornstarch
- ❍ ⅓ cup + 1 Tbsp sugar
- ❍ ¼ tsp salt
- ❍ 2 cups + 2 Tbsp whole milk
- ❍ Seeds from one vanilla bean
- ❍ 2 Tbsp butter

Grease a 9" x 13" pan with Gluten-Free Pan Rub and line with parchment overhanging the sides. Grease the top of the parchment and add parchment overhanging the sides in the other direction. (Greasing the top of the first parchment keeps the second one from sliding around.) You want enough parchment on the sides to give you "handles" to lift the cake out.

Cream the butter and sugar until pale and light-colored. Add egg yolks one at a time, beating thoroughly and scraping the bowl as needed. Add vanilla along with the last egg yolk. Mix flour and baking powder together and then add the mix to the batter. Add milk last and mix thoroughly. Spread the stiff batter in the pan.

Beat egg whites and cream of tartar until soft peaks form. Add sugar gradually, beating at high speed until stiff peaks form. Spread the meringue smoothly on top of the cake batter. Sprinkle with sliced almonds. Bake for 35–40 minutes until a skewer inserted in the middle comes out clean and the meringue is firm. Cool cake completely in the pan on a wire rack.

For the pastry cream, whisk egg, egg yolk, cornstarch, sugar, and salt in a small bowl. Heat milk with vanilla seeds just until boiling. Pour about ⍰ of the milk into the eggs and whisk together. Then add that mixture to the rest of the milk. Bring to a boil and cook about 30 seconds, just until thick. Remove from heat and stir in butter until it melts. Put the custard in a bowl and cover with plastic wrap on the surface of the custard so a skin doesn't form. Chill well before assembling cake.

For the filling, whip the cream and fold into half of the pastry cream. Take the cake out of the pan and cut in half crossways with a serrated knife. Place one half on a plate, top with the filling, and then put the other half on top. You will have a rectangular cake. Chill for at least an hour before serving.

Svensk Äpplekaka

Swedish Apple Cake

There may be as many recipes for Swedish Apple Cake as there are cooks in Sweden. This one is very similar to the apple cake served at IKEA, the famous Swedish store. When I have a chance to shop there, I always go to the cafeteria for a slice of this cake.

Vanilla beans give the best vanilla flavor, but they are expensive. If you don't want to use them in all three parts of this recipe, use them in the custard sauce. You will get the best bang for the buck in terms of flavor there.

Serves 12-16
Oven: 375°F

Crust

❍ 1 cup one-for-one flour
❍ ¼ cup sugar
❍ ⅛ tsp baking soda
❍ ¼ tsp cardamom
❍ Seeds from ½ vanilla bean or 1 ½ tsp vanilla
❍ ½ cup cold butter, cut into pieces
❍ 1 egg

Filling

❍ 2 to 2 ½ lb tart apples, about 6 cups sliced
❍ ½ cup blanched almonds
❍ ½ cup one-for-one flour
❍ ½ cup sugar
❍ ¼ tsp ground cardamom
❍ ⅛ tsp nutmeg
❍ Seeds from ½ vanilla bean or 1 ½ tsp vanilla
❍ ½ cup butter, very soft
❍ 2 eggs, beaten

Vanilla Sauce

- ❍ Seeds from 1 vanilla bean or 1 Tbsp vanilla
- ❍ ½ cup cream
- ❍ ¾ cup whole milk
- ❍ 2 tsp potato starch
- ❍ 2 egg yolks
- ❍ 2 Tbsp sugar

Grease a 10″ springform pan. Combine the dry ingredients for the crust with the seeds from half a vanilla bean. (If using vanilla extract, add that with the egg). Mix thoroughly. Add the butter and mix until the dough forms small crumbs. This is most easily done in a food processor. Add the egg and pulse until the dough is evenly mixed.

Press about ¾ of the dough into the bottom of the pan as evenly as possible.

Refrigerate until you are ready to put the filling in the pan. Wrap the remaining dough in plastic wrap and refrigerate. Preheat the oven to 375°F.

Pulverize the almonds in a food processor or grinder. Peel and slice the apples similar to the way you would for apple pie, but cut the slices in half so you end up with pieces about an inch square or less.

Combine the ground almonds, flour, sugar, and spices in a bowl. Add the seeds from half a vanilla bean and mix in. Add the butter and eggs (and vanilla extract if you aren't using a vanilla bean) and mix until well combined. Fold in the apples. Pour the filling into the prepared cake pan.

Roll out the remaining pastry to about ⅛″ thick and cut out decorative shapes for the top of the cake. They won't cover the entire surface of the cake. Bake for about an hour until the center is set and the top is nicely golden. The cake can be served warm, chilled, or at room temperature.

For the vanilla sauce, place the milk, cream, and seeds from one vanilla bean or vanilla extract in a small saucepan. Heat at a medium-low setting, stirring frequently with a whisk. When it is just beginning to simmer, take it off the heat and let it sit for 15 minutes. DO NOT BOIL. Place a small portion of the cream mixture in a small bowl and add the eggs, sugar, and potato starch. Whisk thoroughly, and then return the egg mixture to the pan with the rest of the cream mixture. Simmer over low heat until the sauce thickens and becomes glossy. DO NOT BOIL. Remove from heat and set aside. It will thicken more as it cools. Serve over the cake, either warm or chilled.

Ostkaka

Swedish Cheesecake

This recipe makes me think it was developed in a time when dairy products were plentiful on every farm, but flour and sugar had to be purchased. It is tangier and less sweet than American cheesecake. I like it for breakfast too (I leave the whipped cream off then).

Serves 8–10
Oven: 350°F

- ❍ 2 eggs
- ❍ ¼ cup one-for-one flour
- ❍ 1 ½ cups half-and-half
- ❍ ½ cup blanched almonds, finely chopped
- ❍ 1 15-oz container ricotta cheese, preferably whole-milk ricotta
- ❍ 2 Tbsp sugar
- ❍ Berries or lingonberry jam and whipped cream for serving

Whisk eggs, flour, and half-and-half together till smooth. Stir in almonds, ricotta, and sugar; mix until well combined. Grease a 1 ½ quart loaf pan and line it with parchment running the long way, with enough parchment to make "handles" at the ends. Pour batter into the pan and bake for 1 hour. The cake should be lightly brown on the edges but with the middle still a bit wobbly. Cool on a rack to room temperature and remove from pan, inverting onto a tray. Chill until served. Serve with berries or jam and whipped cream.

Möndlurkaka
Icelandic Almond Cake

This is one of my go-to recipes when I want to serve something a little different for dessert, and it's easy to make. Traditionally, this recipe would have been made with a jam filling during the cold months and fresh berries in the spring and summer. You can use either filling alone, but I like the combination of jam and fresh berries the best. The jam adds a bit of moisture and a slight tang, and it keeps the sliced strawberries from sliding around. This cake has a different texture than sponge cake because of the ground almonds in the batter, and because of the almonds, it doesn't rise quite as much as a sponge cake would.

Serves 12
Oven: 350°F

<u>Cake</u>

- ❍ 1 cup butter, softened
- ❍ 1 cup sugar
- ❍ 4 eggs, separated
- ❍ 1 tsp vanilla
- ❍ 1 cup ground almonds
- ❍ 1 cup gluten-free flour (containing xanthan gum or not; both work)
- ❍ ¾ tsp baking powder

<u>Filling</u>

- ❍ ½ cup strawberry jam
- ❍ 1 quart fresh strawberries, sliced (Reserve a few for decoration on top.)

<u>Whipped Cream and decoration</u>

- ❍ 1 ½ cups whipping cream
- ❍ 2 Tbsp powdered sugar
- ❍ 1 tsp cornstarch (optional)
- ❍ Fresh strawberries and/or sliced almonds for garnish

Butter three 8″ round cake pans or grease with Gluten-Free Pan Rub and line with parchment. Do not skip the parchment, or the cake won't come out of the pan.

Cream the butter and sugar. Add egg yolks and beat until light and fluffy. Add the vanilla and ground almonds. Mix flour and baking powder together in a small bowl. Mix into the batter. Beat egg whites until stiff and fold into the batter. Divide batter among the pans. Bake for 25–30 minutes or until golden and the cake springs back when touched. If you can't get three pans all on one oven rack, bake them sequentially so that they all bake evenly. Cool on a rack for five minutes and then invert onto rack and finish cooling.

Warm the jam for about 30 seconds in the microwave and stir it. If there are large pieces of strawberry in the jam, it can be sieved to even out the texture. Spread jam on the bottom layer and top with sliced strawberries. Repeat with the second layer. Put the third layer on top. The cake may be covered with plastic wrap at this point if you want to wait to add the whipped cream just before serving.

If you want to stabilize the whipped cream so it will not weep and will hold its shape better, heat ¼ cup of the cream with the cornstarch and the sugar. Bring to a boil and immediately remove from heat. Cool to room temperature and then add to the rest of the cream before whipping. Stabilizing the cream is worthwhile if you want to use a pastry bag with a decorative tip to embellish the cake with the whipped cream. If you don't want to stabilize the cream, just whip it with the sugar until it is stiff. Spread whipped cream on the top and sides of the cake. Decorate the top of the cake with whole or halved fresh strawberries and sliced almonds. Refrigerate until served.

Toscakaka

Caramel and Almond Cake

Norwegians, Swedes, Finns, and Danes all seem to claim this popular cake. The most prevalent theory is that it took its name from the opera Tosca, which premiered in 1900 and in Sweden in 1904. In Sweden, at least, not only cake but race horses and perfume were named Tosca after the opera. This is a fairly quick and easy cake to make, and it goes very well with coffee. It also freezes well.

Serves about 10
Oven: 350°F

Cake

- ❍ 3 eggs
- ❍ 1 cup sugar
- ❍ 1 tsp vanilla
- ❍ 1 ½ cups one-for-one flour
- ❍ 1 ½ tsp baking powder
- ❍ ½ cup butter, melted and cooled
- ❍ 3 Tbsp milk

Topping

- ❍ ⅓ cup butter
- ❍ ½ cup slivered or sliced almonds
- ❍ ½ cup sugar
- ❍ ½ cup whipping cream

Grease a 10″ springform pan or a tart pan with removable bottom. Beat the eggs until they are foamy and add the sugar. Beat until the mixture is lemony in color, then mix in vanilla. Mix the flour and baking powder together in a separate bowl and then fold into to the egg mixture. Mix the butter and milk together and stir into the batter. Pour into the prepared pan and bake for about 35 minutes at 350°F. Cake should be lightly browned on top, and a toothpick inserted in the center should come out clean. Ten to fifteen minutes before the cake is done, begin preparing the topping. Melt the butter in a skillet and then add the almonds. Stir until the almonds begin to look toasted. Add the sugar and cream, and stir well. Turn up the heat and bring to a boil. Boil for about 2 ½ minutes until the mixture has thickened and looks a little bit brown. Pour onto the top of the baked cake just after you remove it from the oven. Turn off the oven and turn the broiler on low. Place the pan on the middle rack of the oven and broil for 2 minutes until the topping is bubbling and a light brown. Cool the cake completely before removing it from the pan. It may be necessary to run a knife around the perimeter of the pan to loosen it before you remove it from the pan. The caramel at the edges can stick the cake pretty firmly to the pan.

Fyrstekake

Prince's Cake

Fyrstekake is also known as Norwegian Royal Cake, although it is more dense than an ordinary cake. It's very simple and not overly sweet, with an almond filling in a rich crust. Fyrstekake is said to date to Trondheim in the 1860s. Fyrstekake is very good with coffee but makes a good dessert after a meal, too. This is another recipe I got from my Norwegian friend Ella many years ago.

Serves 8–10
Oven 375°F

Crust

- ❍ 1 ½ cups one-for-one-flour
- ❍ 1 tsp baking powder
- ❍ 1 tsp xanthan gum
- ❍ ½ cup sugar
- ❍ ½ cup + 1 Tbsp butter
- ❍ 2 egg yolks (use whites in filling)

Filling

- ❍ 1 cup almonds
- ❍ 1 cup powdered sugar
- ❍ 2 egg whites, slightly beaten

Mix dry ingredients together, and add the butter cut into pieces. Pulse in a food processor or blend with a pastry blender until the mixture resembles a coarse flour. Add the egg yolks and mix thoroughly. Chill the dough while making the filling. To make the filling, finely grind the almonds in a food processor and then grind them again with the powdered sugar. Blend thoroughly with the egg whites, beating for several minutes. Chill.

Set aside about one cupful of the crust mixture and pat the rest onto the bottom and sides of an 8″ cake pan. Spread the filling over the crust. Take the remaining crust dough and roll out to ⅛″ thickness. You may need to add up to 1 Tbsp water to get the dough to hang together so it can be rolled. Cut strips ½″ wide and lay 3 each way across the pan to form a lattice. Press an additional ½″ strip around the edge of the cake. The dough is very tender, and the strips may break, but don't worry–they will bake together and look fine. Bake for about 30 minutes until golden brown. Let the cake cool on a rack until it is warm but not hot. Carefully loosen sides and remove from pan. Serve in wedges. You can also make this in a cake or tart pan with a removable bottom.

Other Desserts

Rømmegrøt

Norwegian Cream Pudding

Rømmegrøt means "sour cream pudding," but in the US, it's often made with regular cream. Our commercial sour cream is not the same as unpasteurized cream that sours on its own. The first time I visited Norway, we stayed with a cousin of my mother's on the farm where my grandfather grew up. I was told by another cousin beforehand that we would be served rømmegrøt because our visit was special and that I had better eat it! That wasn't a problem because it was so yummy. This is a very modern recipe that is cooked in the microwave. It's a nice alternative to long cooking times on the stovetop that require continuous stirring. The traditional mode of preparation involved cooking the cream and flour until the butter separated and rose to the top. This recipe uses a combination of whole milk and butter instead of cream.

Makes 2 ½ to 3 cups
Serves 8–10

- ❍ 2 cups whole milk
- ❍ 1 cup one-for-one flour (SEE NOTE)
- ❍ ½ cup butter
- ❍ ¼ cup sugar
- ❍ ½ tsp salt
- ❍ Butter and cinnamon for serving

Heat milk to scalding (180°F or until a skin forms on top). Set aside. Melt the butter in a microwave-safe bowl. Whisk the butter into the flour and then mix in the sugar and salt. Add the hot milk and whisk until the biggest lumps are gone. Microwave in 30-second intervals, whisking after each one until the mixture is thick and smooth (1–2 minutes total). Serve warm with a dab of butter and a sprinkle of cinnamon on top.

NOTE: I do not recommend using Namaste flour for this recipe. The pudding was lumpy and grainy in texture, and it had an off-color.

Riskrem

Rice Pudding

This recipe is naturally gluten free because it requires no flour. I include it because Riskrem is a staple on many Christmas Eve tables. The Swedish tradition is to hide a whole almond in the pudding. Whoever ends up with the almond will be the next to marry. My Sons of Norway lodge always serves it on the 17th of May (Norway's Constitution Day).

Serves 8-10

Pudding

- ❍ 1 ½ cups rice
- ❍ 3 cups water
- ❍ 1 tsp salt
- ❍ 2 quarts whole milk
- ❍ ½ cup sugar
- ❍ ½ to 1 cup whipping cream

Raspberry sauce (optional)

- ❍ 2 cups raspberries, fresh or frozen
- ❍ ¾ cup sugar
- ❍ ½ cup water
- ❍ ½ tsp vanilla
- ❍ 2 tsp cornstarch
- ❍ 2 Tbsp water
- ❍ 1 Tbsp butter

Cook the rice in salted water until all the water is absorbed, about 20 minutes. Then add the milk and cook for 1-2 hours over very low heat, stirring occasionally until all the milk is absorbed. This step can also be done in a slow cooker with the cover off. This *risgrøt* [rice porridge] can be eaten as-is, with a sprinkling of sugar and cinnamon. For *riskrem,* stir in sugar and cream until the pudding is your desired consistency. The amount of cream you add will depend on how much milk has already been absorbed by the rice, and how thick you like your Riskrem. Some eat this with sugar and cinnamon too, but it is also often topped with a dollop of raspberry sauce.

To make the sauce: Mix the cornstarch and 2 Tbsp water and set aside. In a saucepan over medium heat, stir together the raspberries, sugar, and water. Heat to boiling, stirring often. Reduce heat and add the vanilla. Add cornstarch slurry to the hot raspberry mixture. Boil over medium heat, stirring often, for about 4 minutes until thickened. Remove from heat and stir in the butter. If you wish, you can puree the sauce in a blender. Refrigerate until used.

Quick Breads and Flatbreads

Æbleskiver

Danish Pancake Balls

"Æble" means "apple." These pancake balls are traditionally made with an apple filling or served with applesauce on the side. Unfilled æbleskiver are also frequently served sprinkled with powdered sugar, with jam on the side. There are dozens of variations out there and even entire cookbooks devoted solely to æbleskiver. So really, you can fill these with any kind of jam or with Nutella. Apple butter is also good. I prefer them with some kind of filling inside rather than plain with applesauce on the side. These are best served warm. Unless you are home alone, you won't have many leftovers, but they are good when cool too.

Æbleskiver are made in a pan with hemispherical wells. Traditional pans are cast iron for the stovetop, but electric ones are also available.

About 2 dozen

Pancakes

- ❍ 3 eggs, separated
- ❍ 1 ¼ cups buttermilk SEE NOTE
- ❍ ⅓ cup cream
- ❍ 1 Tbsp sugar
- ❍ 1 tsp vanilla
- ❍ 1 tsp baking powder
- ❍ ½ tsp baking soda
- ❍ ½ tsp salt
- ❍ 1 tsp cardamom
- ❍ 1 ¾ cups one-for-one flour (SEE NOTE)
- ❍ 3 Tbsp butter, melted, for greasing pan

Filling

- ❍ 2–3 medium apples, peeled, cored, diced (to make 2 ½ to 3 cups)
- ❍ ⅓ cup butter
- ❍ ⅓ cup brown sugar

Start with the filling. Melt the butter and brown sugar together in a skillet. Add the apples and cook until the apples are tender and liquid has cooked off. Drain in a sieve if there is still liquid remaining. Cool to room temperature.

Mix the flour, baking powder, soda, salt, and cardamom together and set aside. In another bowl, mix the egg yolks, buttermilk, cream, vanilla, and sugar. Add the dry ingredients and mix gently until combined. In a separate bowl, beat the egg whites until stiff. Fold egg whites into the batter and put it in the fridge to rest for 30 minutes. This allows the buttermilk to react with the soda to produce lots of bubbles that make the batter really light.

The pan is hot enough when a drop of water will dance on it. Brush the wells with melted butter. Put about a tablespoon of batter in a well, add about half a teaspoon of filling, and then another tablespoon of batter and seal in the filling. The total amount of batter should be below the top of the well; if there is too much batter, it is difficult to bake these all the way through. When bubbles form on the top of the batter, turn with wooden skewers, a fork, or knitting needles (the traditional way) until nicely browned all the way around (3–4 minutes total). Brush the wells with melted butter each time before adding batter.

Keep warm in a 200°F oven. Sprinkle with powdered sugar before serving. Makes about 2 dozen.

<u>NOTE</u>: If you are using powdered buttermilk, mix 5 Tbsp buttermilk powder with the dry ingredients, and add 1 ¼ cups water to the egg yolks.

I do not recommend making these with Domata flour. When made with Domata flour, which contains cornstarch as the second-most abundant ingredient, the æbleskiver tasted okay, but the texture was chewy rather than tender. Although Cup4Cup also lists cornstarch as the second-most abundant ingredient, the percentage of cornstarch is apparently less since Cup4Cup works fine in this recipe.

Pönnukökur

Icelandic Pancakes

Pönnukökur are small, crepe-like pancakes that are filled with sugar and rolled up. My kids loved to visit their dad's Icelandic aunts, Jóna and Ágústa, because we would always be served pönnukökur. Both of these dear women would often have some in their freezers. If not, the pan would come out, and before we knew it, we were gobbling these up. These are best eaten warm, but they taste good at room temperature too. Don't worry if they don't turn out perfectly round; they will taste just fine anyway. Sometimes I end up with pönnukökur that look more like a map of Iceland than a circle, but the eaters never complain.

Makes 3–3 ½ dozen

- ❍ 2 eggs
- ❍ ⅓ cup sugar
- ❍ ¼ tsp salt
- ❍ ½ tsp cinnamon
- ❍ 1 tsp vanilla
- ❍ ½ tsp baking soda
- ❍ ½ cup sour cream or buttermilk
- ❍ 1 tsp baking powder
- ❍ 1 ½ cups one-for-one flour (SEE NOTE)
- ❍ 2 cups milk
- ❍ Mixture of half white sugar, half brown sugar for filling
- ❍ Butter for greasing pan

Beat the eggs and add sugar, salt, vanilla, and cinnamon. Dissolve soda in about a teaspoonful of hot water and mix it with the sour cream or buttermilk. Add that to the egg mixture and mix well. Measure flour and baking powder in a separate bowl and mix well together, then add to the batter. Mix well until there are no lumps. Gradually mix in the milk. The batter will be thin and runny. I usually use a hand mixer for this.

Use a fairly heavy griddle pan on medium to medium-high heat. Rub the bottom of the pan with a bit of butter; this is easiest to do if the butter is wrapped in cheesecloth. Lift the pan off the heat and quickly pour about ⍰ cup batter in the center of the pan. Swirl the pan around to distribute the batter as thinly as possible, making a round pancake about 4–5″ in diameter. Put the pan back on the stove. As soon as the bottom is golden brown, which may be right away, flip the pancake over and cook until the second side is golden brown. Rub pan with more butter before repeating. Fill these with a mixture of brown and white sugar, roll them up, and eat warm if at all possible. These can be frozen. Bring to room temperature before serving. You cannot warm them in the microwave, or all the sugar filling will melt.

<u>NOTE:</u> Do not use Domata or Cup4Cup flour for this recipe. The high cornstarch content in these two flours thickens the batter excessively, and you cannot make a thin pancake with it. Do not use Namaste flour either because the arrowroot in it also thickens the batter too much.

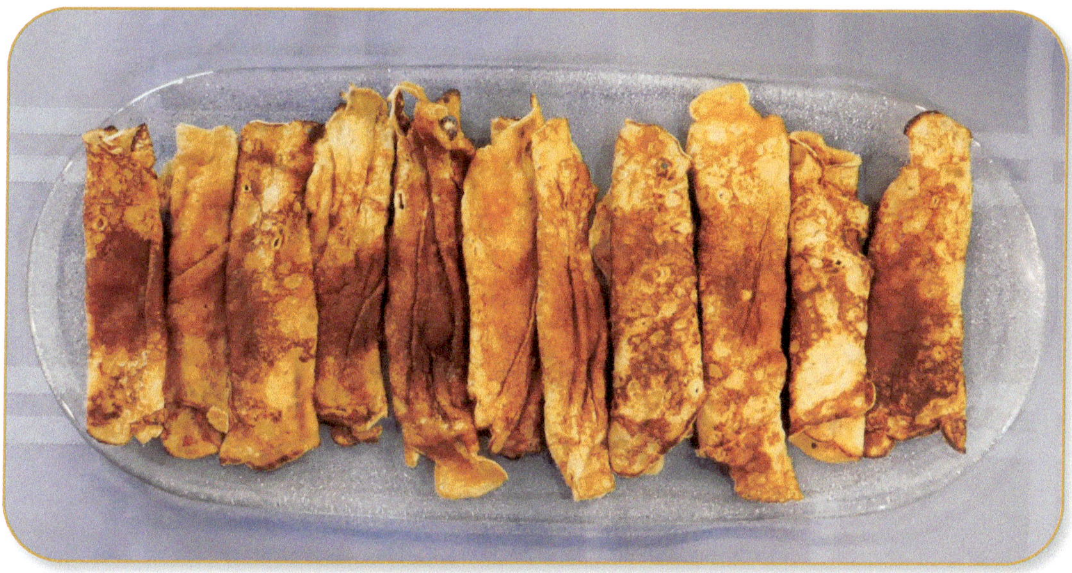

Norsk Waffler
Norwegian Waffles

Heart-shaped waffles are a common snack all around Norway. I recall seeing them at the concession stand outside the Viking Ship Museum and also at the North Cape visitors' center. They are thinner and eggier than American breakfast waffles. I got this recipe from a Norwegian friend more than forty years ago.

Makes about 5 waffles approx. 6" in diameter

- ❍ 2 eggs
- ❍ ¼ cup sugar
- ❍ 1 ½ cups one-for-one flour
- ❍ ½ tsp baking powder
- ❍ ½ tsp salt
- ❍ ⅜ cup water (6 Tbsp)
- ❍ 1 ½ cups milk
- ❍ 4 Tbsp butter, melted and cooled
- ❍ ½ tsp cardamom

Mix the dry ingredients together in a small bowl. Beat the eggs and sugar, then add the butter and mix in. Add the dry ingredients alternately with the liquid and mix well. Let batter stand for about 30 minutes after mixing. Heat the waffle iron until a drop of water will jump from the surface. Use about ⅔ cup of batter per waffle; adjust amount to suit your waffle iron. Bake until golden brown.

Serve with strawberry jam and whipped cream or with Norwegian brown cheese or both. These can be eaten either warm or at room temperature.

Lefse

Norwegian Potato Flatbread

There has always been a debate in my extended family about whether lefse is best with just butter or with butter and sugar. The question even came up on my first date with my husband! Either way, it is a necessary part of our family's menu for Thanksgiving and Christmas. Like all lefse, this is at its best when eaten warm off the griddle! Make lots so there is enough for the big meal after everyone in the family does "quality control testing" while you are making it.

Lefse can be refrigerated for a couple of days or frozen. This is not quite as supple as regular lefse when rewarmed to room temperature, but if you microwave it for a moment, it will be softer and less likely to crack when rolled up to eat.

Russet potatoes are best for this because they are higher in starch and lower in water content than red potatoes. If you use red potatoes, you will probably need more flour, and your lefse may not be quite as tender.

Makes about 24 10" rounds

- ❍ 5 lb russet potatoes
- ❍ 1 cup whipping cream
- ❍ 2 Tbsp butter at room temperature
- ❍ Approx. 2 cups one-for-one flour, divided, plus additional for rolling
- ❍ 1 tsp salt
- ❍ 4 tsp xanthan gum, divided

Peel the potatoes and boil in salted water until they are fork-tender. Drain and allow to dry for a few minutes. Put boiled potatoes through a ricer. (You can mash them, but you are likely to end up with lumps, which create flaws in the lefse.) Mix riced potatoes with the cream, butter, and salt using a hand mixer. Do not overmix, or you will cause the starch to become gluey, and it will result in tough lefse. Cover and chill the mashed potatoes for several hours or overnight so the cream and butter can combine with the starch in the potatoes.

Mix one cup flour with 2 tsp xanthan gum. Add to half the mashed potatoes. Mix well (hands work best for this). Roll into a log and slice into twelve sections, each about the size of a hamburger. Cover pastry cloth with some additional flour. Take a piece of dough, pat it out with hands to flatten, and turn to cover with flour on both sides. Roll with a well-floured, stockinette-covered lefse rolling pin until about 10 inches in diameter. Lift carefully with lefse stick and bake on an ungreased griddle at 375°F, turning when underside develops some nice brown freckles. If the lefse tears when picked up, it probably needs a bit more flour. Roll it into a ball, add a teaspoon or so of flour, and pat and roll out again. Lay the baked lefse round on a cotton dishtowel, and cover with another towel. Repeat with remaining dough sections, layering a towel between each lefse. If you don't let them steam like this until cool, they will get hard and crisp. Let stand until all lefse are cool. Repeat with the second half of the dough. Refrigerate or freeze. Serve at room temperature. These 10″ rounds of lefse are usually cut in thirds for serving. Smaller ones can be cut in half.

Julekake

Christmas Bread

My mother and her mother made large batches of yeast-raised julekake every year before Christmas. I especially like it for breakfast on Christmas morning. Julekake made with yeast takes several hours to rise because the heavy fruit makes the dough very slow to rise, even when made with very high-gluten flour. I have not found a good gluten-free recipe that uses yeast. (Many attempts ended up in the garbage!) This is an excellent alternative to yeast-raised julekake, and it takes much less time. This recipe is adapted from my grandma's yeast-raised recipe. It's good toasted, too.

Makes one large round loaf
Oven: 375°F

<u>Dough</u>

- ❍ 1 ½ tsp salt
- ❍ ½ cup granulated sugar
- ❍ ½ tsp cinnamon
- ❍ 3 ½ cups one-for-one flour (SEE NOTE)
- ❍ 4 tsp baking powder
- ❍ ¾ cup candied fruit (fruit cake mix), 5-6 ounces
- ❍ ¼ cup raisins
- ❍ ⅓ cup maraschino cherries, drained and patted dry
- ❍ 1 ¼ cups milk at room temperature
- ❍ 4 Tbsp butter, melted and cooled
- ❍ 3 eggs, one separated (reserve white)
- ❍ ½ tsp almond extract

<u>Glaze</u>

- ❍ 1 egg white
- ❍ 1 Tbsp sugar
- ❍ Pearl sugar

Coat an 8″ diameter, 3″ deep pan with Gluten-Free Pan Rub.

Mix dry ingredients together in a large bowl and add the candied fruit, raisins, and maraschino cherries. Dredge the fruit in the flour mixture. Whisk together the two eggs and one yolk with the milk, butter, and almond extract. Add the liquid ingredients to the dry mixture and stir well until there are no bits of white flour showing on the fruit. Put the dough in the pan and smooth the top. Whip the egg white and sugar together until just frothy. Apply the glaze with a pastry brush (you will not use all of it) and sprinkle with pearl sugar. If you want to put icing on the top as some people do, brush the dough with the egg white mixture, but skip the pearl sugar, and add icing after the bread has cooled.

Bake for 60–65 minutes until nicely browned on top and a skewer inserted in the middle comes out clean. Cool on a rack for about 15 minutes and then remove from pan.

NOTE: When made with Bob's Red Mill 1:1 flour, the julekake had a slight "whole grain" flavor, and the bread was a light tan, not white. It was acceptable, but other flours that don't contain garbanzo bean flour gave better flavor.

Hafrakex

Icelandic Oatmeal Biscuits

This recipe is adapted from one in a 1988 cookbook published by the Leif Eiriksson Icelandic Club in Calgary, Alberta. The recipe originated with a woman in Borgarfirði, Iceland. These are sweeter and heartier than a plain baking powder biscuit. This is one of those instances where the gluten-free dough needs to rest before the biscuits can be cut. If you skip this step, the biscuits will have a gritty texture.

Makes 10–12
Oven: 400°F

- ❍ 2 cups one-for-one flour
- ❍ 1 cup old-fashioned rolled oats
- ❍ ½ cup sugar
- ❍ 1 Tbsp baking powder
- ❍ ½ cup butter, room temperature
- ❍ ¾ cup milk

Mix the dry ingredients and then cut in the butter. Add milk and stir to form a dough. Turn out onto a floured surface and knead a few times to create a cohesive mass of dough. Cover with a towel and let rest 30 minutes. Pat or roll out to about ½" thick. Cut with a biscuit cutter. Bake on a greased or parchment-lined baking sheet for 17–19 minutes.

Best served warm, but good cool, too. These keep for several days in a sealed container.

Tables

Table 1: Ingredients in Eight Gluten-Free Flours

	Bob's Red Mill All-Purpose Flour	Bobs Red Mill 1:1 Baking Flour	Cup4Cup Flour	Glutino	King Arthur Measure for Measure Flour	Good & Gather GF Flour Blend	Domata Recipe Ready Flour	Namaste Perfect Flour Blend
Rice Flour*					x	x	x	
White Rice Flour*				x	x			
Sweet White Rice Flour*		x						
Brown Rice Flour*		x						x
Whole Grain Brown Rice Flour*					x			
Rice Flour Blend			x					
Sweet Brown Rice Flour								x
Millet Flour						x		
Potato Starch	x	x	x	x	x	x		
Tapioca Starch or Flour**	x	x	x	x	x	x		x
Tapioca Dextrin							x	
Corn Starch			x				x	
Arrowroot Starch								x
Milk Powder			x					
Pea Hull Flour				x				
Garbanzo Bean Flour	x							
Fava Bean Flour	x							
White Sorghum Flour		x	x		x		x	x
Rice Protein				x				
Rice Extract							x	
Cellulose					x			
Acacia Gum				x				
Xanthan Gum		x	x		x	x	x	x
Vitamin & Mineral Blend					x			

* "Rice flour" is made from long or medium grain rice. "Sweet rice flour" is made from short grain rice. It has a much higher starch content. Brown rice flour is made by grinding the rice without removing the bran layer.
* **Tapioca flour and tapioca starch are the same thing.

Table 2: Nutrient Content of Nine Gluten-Free Flours [Based on 30 Grams or about 3 Tablespoons for Each Serving]

	Bob's Red Mill All-Purpose	Bob's Red Mill 1:1	Cup4Cup	Glutino	King Arthur Measure for Measure	King Arthur All Purpose	Domata Recipe Ready	Good & Gather Flour Blend	Namaste Perfect Flour Blend	Daily Value
Calories	106	105	104	96	107	89	107	111	98	
Total Fat (g)	0.4	0	0	0	0	0	0	0.6	0	78
Sodium (mg)	0	8	0	0	0	0	0	11	0	2,300
Total Carbohydrate (g)	22	24	24	22	2	19	26	23	22	275
Protein (g)	2.6	1.6	2.3	2.1	2	0.8	1.1	2.2	1.3	50
Calcium (mg)	11	3	35	26	78	62	21	0	0	1,300
Iron (mg)	0.9	0	0.2	0.7	1.8	0.8	0	1.2	0.7	18
Potassium (mg)	164	48	58	0	NR	24	16	56	0	4,700
Thiamine (mg)	NR	NR	NR	NR	0.16	0.15	NR	NR	NR	1.2
Riboflavin (mg)	NR	NR	NR	NR	0.9	0.1	NR	NR	NR	1.3
Niacin (mg)	NR	NR	NR	NR	1.4	1.5	NR	NR	NR	16

Gram (g): One gram is about 0.035 ounces, about the weight of a paper clip or one raisin.

Milligram (mg): $^{1}/_{1000}$ of a gram.

NR: Not Reported. You can safely assume it is zero or a trivial amount.

Daily Value: Daily value is the amount of a food component used on food nutrition labels. Daily value is usually expressed as a percent of the recommended amount for someone consuming a 2,000-calorie diet. The values highlighted in yellow show amounts that exceed 5 percent of the daily value for that nutrient. Values are for adults and children four years and over. For total fat, sodium, and total carbohydrates, the daily values are recommended upper limits of intake. For the other nutrients listed, the daily values are recommended daily intakes. That means you should aim to reach or exceed that level each day.

ABOUT THE AUTHOR

I began baking at the age of five when my mother gave me a cake mix that had the directions "beat [by hand] 50 strokes." I now have seventy years of baking experience, which includes passing the "Can she bake a cherry pie, Billy Boy?" test without a cookbook when I went to meet a boyfriend's parents. My mother and both grandmothers were superb bakers who taught me to make lots of Scandinavian goodies.

I am of Norwegian and Swedish descent, and I grew up celebrating holidays and special occasions with a variety of ethnic goodies, learning how to make many of them from my grandmothers. My first husband was of Icelandic descent, and I learned to prepare a variety of Icelandic recipes from his mother and aunts.

I have a PhD in chemistry, had an internationally recognized research career in human clinical nutrition, and became a senior executive at the United States Department of Agriculture's Agricultural Research Service. As the director of USDA's largest and most comprehensive research center, I had to be knowledgeable about a wide range of scientific disciplines, including nutrition, food science, and food safety. My background in chemistry and nutrition has been extremely helpful in making successful gluten-free modifications of traditional recipes.

In 1988, I was elected the first female District President of the Sons of Norway in the then ninety years of the organization's existence. I went on to join the Board of Directors of Sons of Norway International for a four-year term. I have been a member of Gyda Varden Lodge in Grand Forks, North Dakota, since 1975. I have traveled to Norway, Iceland, Sweden, Denmark, and Finland several times. Travel has given me the opportunity to experience Scandinavian baking firsthand.